PETERS FRASER & DUNLOP

5TH FLOOR
THE CHAMBERS
CHELSEA HARBOUR, LOTS ROAD
LONDON SW10 0XF

TELEPHONE 01-376 7878
FAX 01-352 7356
TELEX 28965 SCRIPT G

Lucky

ROGER McGOUGH

Lucky

A Book of Poems

Illustrated by Sally Kindberg

VIKING

VIKING

Published by the Penguin Group
Penguin Books Ltd, 27 Wrights Lane, London W8 5TZ, England
Penguin Books USA Inc., 375 Hudson Street, New York, New York 10014, USA
Penguin Books Australia Ltd, Ringwood, Victoria, Australia
Penguin Books Canada Ltd, 10 Alcorn Avenue, Toronto, Ontario, Canada M4V 3B2
Penguin Books (NZ) Ltd, 182–190 Wairau Road, Auckland 10, New Zealand

Penguin Books Ltd, Registered Offices: Harmondsworth, Middlesex, England

First published 1993
1 3 5 7 9 10 8 6 4 2
First edition

Filmset in Linotronic 12pt Bembo

Printed in England by Clays Ltd, St Ives plc

A CIP catalogue record for this book is available from the British Library

ISBN 0-670-84619-8

Contents

Lucky

There was a boy at school we called 'Lucky'
  All he did was whinge and moan
'Lucky' was the nickname we gave him
  Because he was so accident-prone

If something was spilled or knocked over
  Splattered, burnt or bust
There in the midst of the damage
  Would be Lucky looking nonplussed

He said that bad things happened to him
  Having been born under an unlucky star
And a fortune-teller warned his mother
  Not to let him travel far

So to ward off every kind of harm
  The gypsy gave him a lucky charm:
A silver horseshoe, rabbit's paw,
  Lucky heather, eagle's claw,
Coloured glass and polished stones
  Dried hair and yellowing bones

He never walked under ladders
  Never stepped on pavement cracks
Never touched a looking-glass
  Never learned how to relax

You could spot Lucky a mile off
  Count the creases in his frown
As he concentrated on keeping alive
  His pockets weighted down

With a silver horseshoe, rabbit's paw,
  Lucky heather, eagle's claw,
Coloured glass and polished stones
  Dried hair and yellowing bones

Though the streets were full of happy kids
  He was never allowed out to play
In case of bombs, or tigers, or ghosts
  So he stayed in, out of harm's way

Then one afternoon his luck changed
  (Friday the Thirteenth, coincidentally)
He'd been kept in detention after school
  For setting fire to it (accidentally)

When hurrying home and touching wood
  For it was then well after dark
Three lads jumped him, mugged him
  Took all he had, near the gates of the park

A silver horseshoe, rabbit's paw,
  Lucky heather, eagle's claw,
Coloured glass and polished stones
  Dried hair and yellowing bones

Lucky laid low and cowered for days
    As if some tragedy would befall
But nothing unusual happened
    Nothing. Simply nothing at all

It was as if he'd been living underwater
    And at last had come up for air
Then the following week his dad won the pools
    And became a millionaire

We never saw Lucky after that
    The family moved out to Australia
So the moral is: Chuck them away
    Or doomed you'll be to failure

A silver horseshoe, rabbit's paw,
    Lucky heather, eagle's claw,
Coloured glass and polished stones
    Dried hair and yellowing bones

Class Warfare

I'm the most important
Person in the class

Twenty-four carat diamond
While all the rest are glass

Distinctions distinguish me
While others strive to pass

I'm en route for glory
While others are en masse

They're backdrops, they're bit parts
They're day-old candy floss

They provide the undercoat
For my enduring gloss

When I go down in history
I'll go down a storm

For I'm the most important
Person in the form

(If you don't believe me
Ask Daddy — he's the headmaster.)

Dear Sir,

I wish to apply for the post of pizza topping
consultant. As I am very fond of pizzas and
enjoy the company of people, I believe I would be
most suitable. The job, as I understand it, would
be to talk to customers in depth, getting to know
their likes and dislikes, dreams and aspirations,
background, education, star signs and the like.
Using the information, I would then advise them
on the topping best suited to their character.

I would be willing either to work in the
restaurant itself, or to visit the homes of
prospective customers who prefer to choose
from your extensive take-away menu.

Although unemployed for the last seventeen
years, prior to that I was at school.

Yours faithfully

A. Lacey

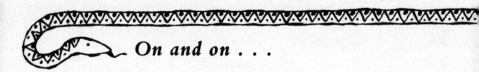

On and on . . .

Is a well-wisher
  someone
who wishes at a well?

Is a bad speller
  one
who casts a wicked spell?

Is a shop-lifter
  a giant
who goes around lifting shops?

Is a popsinger
  someone
who sings and then pops?

Is a fly fisherman
  an angler
who fishes for flies?

Is an eye-opener
  a gadget
for opening eyes?

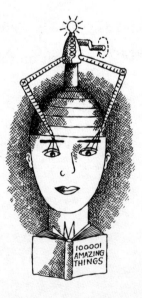

Is a night nurse
　a nurse
who looks after the night?

Who puts it to bed
　and then
turns off the light?

Is a big spender
　a spendthrift
who is exceedingly big?

Is a pig farmer
　really
a land-owning pig?

Does a baby-sitter
　really
sit on tiny tots?

Is a pot-holer
　a gunman
who shoots holes in pots?

Gourmet Corner

Went out
to dine:
Chicken à
la King

The sauce
was fine.
The chicken?
Lacking

Rasta Pasta

Spaghetti with ganja sauce.

Jack Pratt

I like my food insipid
Tasteless, mawkish, flat
Vapid, wishy-washy
Yum Yum I like all that

My wife, now she likes spices
Pungent, stinging hot
Peppery, biting, racy
(We don't eat out a lot).

Drinking Song

Drink wine
Think romance
You're a lover

Feel fine
Sing and dance
Fall over.

Minutiae on the Bounty

paperclips
on a chocolate bar.

No Peas for the Wicked

No peas for the wicked
No carrots for the damned
No parsnips for the naughty
O Lord we pray

No sprouts for the shameless
No cabbage for the shady
No lettuce for the lecherous
No way, no way

No potatoes for the deviants
No radish for the riff-raff
No spinach for the spineless
Lock them away

No beetroot for the boasters
No mange-tout for the mobsters
No corn-on-the-cob et cetera
(Shall we call it a day?)

The Big Blow-out

We were driving along
when suddenly
one of the tyres burst

So we stopped
and had a huge meal.

Roll

During the night
his stomach
rolled ominously

off the bed.

The Burp

One evening at supper
A little girl burped.
'Tut tut,' said mother.
'What do you say?' said father.

Her brother giggled.
'It's not funny,' said father.
'Pardon,' said the little girl.
'That's better,' said mother.

And all was quickly forgotten.
Except, that is, by the burp.
It had only just been born
And already everybody was apologizing.

What sort of person gives birth
And then says 'Pardon'?
What sort of relative giggles
Then looks away embarrassed?

Hurt, the baby burp hovered near the ceiling
Looked down at the one who had brought it up
Then escaped through an open window
Never to return.

The Burp II

Like a balloon freed from its skin
the little burp floated high above
the rooftops of London. At the beck
and call of every flick of wind
it toss-tailed over, looped the loop
and zigzagged down to the Thames.

It was a clear night, and the moon
danced on a tightrope of fairylights
reflected in the black velvety water.
Taking a deep breath, the burp
swooped beneath Battersea Bridge
and across the surface of the river.

Skimming soundlessly through Chelsea
it bobbed through Pimlico and beyond
past the palace at Lambeth, beneath Big Ben
until, on reaching Waterloo, felt its energy
draining away. Soon it would be time.
Gravely, it steered itself toward the shore.

Beneath the arches of the Embankment
figures lay huddled like crumpled litter
and in the flickering shadows against the wall
an old man, more tattered than most, lay sleeping.
What the burp saw was a mouth, wide open
and so was drawn toward it, and entered.

Suddenly the old man's dreams tasted good.
Of sarsaparilla and ice-cream, sponge puddings
aglow with syrup. He gulped them down
those tastes of childhood long since past.
Then snuggling down in his cardboard box
he licked his lips, and breathed his last.

Washed Up

When we were born
We were out of our depth
Now we are all adrift

Adrift, adrift
On a cardboard raft
Now we are all adrift

★ ★ ★

When we were young
We were all at sea
Now we are all washed up

Washed up, washed up
On a pavement cold
Old, and all washed up.

Deed for the Day

Helped a blind man across the road
My good deed for the day
Saw him later, agitated
Looked the other way.

. . . *and on* . . .

Is a tree surgeon
   a doctor
made out of wood?

Is a blood donor
   pitta bread
stuffed with blood?

Is an all-rounder
   an athlete
who is completely round?

Is a sound engineer
   one
who is completely sound?

Is a monster crane
   a ferocious
man-eating crane?

Is a train-spotter
   an artist
who paints spots on a train?

Is a cardsharper
   a craftsman
who sharpens cards?

Who guards women
   when
a guardsman guards?

Is a batsman
   a man
who is completely bats?

Is a cat burglar
   a thief
who likes stealing cats?

Is a flat tyre
   a tyre
that you keep in a flat?

Is a hat-trick
   a method
of stealing a hat?

All in Time to the Music

The sea is outrageous
it rages and rages
All in time to the music

Manacled to the moon
for ages and ages
All in time to the music

The sea's a born loser
as old as Methuselah
All in time to the music

A bragger, a swaggerer
gave birth to Niagara
All in time to the music

The sea is secretive
its soul unassailable
All in time to the music

With mountains of water
black and unscalable
All in time to the music

The sea is stricken
terribly sick
All in time to the music

Its arteries thicken
acid and slick
All in time to the music

The sea's in a panic
unstable and manic
All in time to the music

The earth in its clutches
For everything touches
All in time
All in time
All in time to the music

All in time
All in time
All in time to the music.

Morning Has Broken

Morning has broken . . .
Too late the billion gallons of sun lotion
Smeared over the earth's surface
The straw hat covering three continents
Too late the sunglasses wrapped around the equator
The giant space parasol
Too late the ozone elastoplast

Morning has broken . . .
Is it too late to mend it?

Borrowed Time

Apparently we are all living
On Borrowed Time.
What I want to know is
Who borrowed it, and from whom?

And another thing . . .
If we give it back
Can we borrow another?

Dear Sir,

I wish to apply for a job as umpire in the
forthcoming tennis tournament at Wimbledon. I
would not be averse to learning the rules, but,
best of all, I would not take no lip from no
noncey foreign player. What the referee says
goes, or you're dogmeat.

At present I am employed as doorman at the
Golden Parrot Club in Deptford.

I remain, your humble and obedient servant

A. Armstrong

The Mugger's Return

Returns
Goes to toilet
Does not wash hands
Puts mugging money into muggen money-box
Punches mother goodnight
Then turns in
To bad dream.

Advance Planning

January	Relax
February	Take it easy
March	Put feet up
April	Lie doggo
May	Potter about
June	Read a little
July	Sunbathe (within reason)
August	Sunbathe (as above)
September	Rest after sunbathing
October	Kick leaves
November	Rest after kicking leaves
December	Keep warm

Late autumn, while playing
Near the Abbey ruins, I found
What appeared to be a horseshoe
Half buried in the ground

Or it might have been a doorhandle
Or part of some ancient machine
So I stuck it in my schoolbag
And took it home to clean

It was pitted with rust and covered
With mud and molten tar
But I scrubbed until it shone as bright
As a sheriff's silver star

When, lo and behold, a magnet
That fitted neatly in my palm
And holding it then I felt
A sense of overwhelming calm

With a confidence running through me
That I'd never felt before
Without a word to anyone
I slipped out through the door

Walked down the street and out of town
Along the woodland track
Across the valley and over the hill
Not once did I look back

Holding it out before me
Like a diviner seeking gold
I followed the path to Devil's Crag
By destiny made bold

Drawn toward the darkness
Like a medieval alchemist
Deeper I went into the moor
Where the lolling tongue of the mist

Licked my flesh with an icy coldness
As I stumbled half asleep
The magnet pulling harder now
As if a rendezvous to keep

My partner called a livelier tune
I jigged as in a trance
When a clap of thunder, out of time
Stopped my foolish dance

Destiny took to its heels
And from then on I was frightened
The more I tried to free myself
The more my fingers tightened

Then I tripped. But still the magnet
Dragged me through the gorse
Like an Indian brave whose hands are tied
To a wild runaway horse

The wind on my back was screaming
And digging in its claws
As an eerie power drew me
Across the endless moors

Then a thought came that chilled me
As my strength began to fail
Was it Satan there before me?
Did I have him by the tail?

Straight through the windscreen
Of that nightmare I was thrown
And lay at the foot of Devil's Crag
But no longer alone

A hump-backed beast stood over me
It kicked me in the head
Then snatched the metal from my hand
And left me there for dead

No one believed my story
Though my temple bears the proof
A purple stain that will not fade
In the shape of a cloven hoof.

. . . *and on* . . .

Is a rain hood
  a gangster
who sings in the rain?

Will a pain-killer
  kill you
in terrible pain?

Is a tail-gunner
  a gunner
with a big long tail?

Do shoppers buy
  giants
in a giant sale?

Does a lightning conductor
  conduct
orchestras fast?

Is a past master
  a master
who has mastered the past?

Is a light bulb
  a bulb
that is light as a feather?

Does an opera buff
  sing
in the altogether?

Is a fire bucket
  a bucket
that bursts into flames?

Is a gamesmanship
  where sailors
go to play games?

Is a dinner lady
  what cannibals
eat for their dinner?

If you eat your words
  will you
grow thinner?

Meet the Cats

I

Allison has allergies
With dizzy spells and wheezes
The sort of puss
Who makes a fuss
Cries: 'There's a man in the room,'
Then sneezes.

II

Marvo, magician extraordinaire
Can juggle and keep seventeen mice in the air
Audiences roar: 'Encore, encore,'
At the sight of this conjuror's sleight-of-paw.

III

There's many a cat in the cats' *Who's Who*
Who rue the cat they once did woo

From Felixstow to Edinbraw
Titled toms have held her paw

Miaowed her praises, sworn true love
By the light of the milky moon above

Alone now Miranda mopes in her flat
An ex-sex-kitten now a tired old cat.

IV

Thomasina Tittletat
Although a lean
And little cat
Has a tongue as juicy
Long and fat
As a gossip column.

And because of that
Is the uncrowned queen
Of catty chat.

Ash Yew

Cocksfoot, timothy
Dandelion, daisy
Beloved of poets
They drive me crazy

Hazel, laburnum
Ash, yew,
Silver birch, elder
ASH------Y O O O O O.

Every Little Breeze

Every little breeze
Makes me want to sneeze
I can't stand the
countryside in June

When the blossom bursts
in May
I'm going far away
Antarctica or, better still,
the moon.

Colin

My name's Colin
I'm a pollen
My job's to pollinate

On my way to a rose
If I get up your nose
That's where the wind blows, mate.

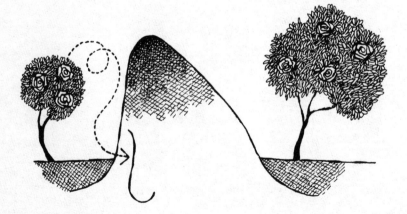

The Death of Nelson

Lord Nelson, though man as man can be
Suffered from hayfever, even at sea

The French knew this and that is why
They attacked when the pollen count was high

Midst the heat and the dust and the cannonsmoke
The allergy struck – he started to choke

In the noonday sun on the Spanish seas
He let go one almighty sneeze

Then sneezed from the fo'c's'le to the stern
(Some folks'll never learn)

His good eye streaming in a wheezing fit
When a musket ball scored a direct hit

I never believed that 'kiss me' stuff
From the lips of an Englishman, heroic and tough

As he sneezed his last he was misheard to say:
'Bless me, Hardy,' then passed away.

Dear Sir or Madam,

Isn't it about time you found another little girl to model for you before the real programmes start? (The one where she sits holding a teddy-bear in front of those coloured squares.) Our Dawn is getting on for seven and is much prettier than the toffee-nosed one you regularly use. Also, she can sit very still when made to (especially by her dad, who is a bouncer at the Greasy Parrot Club in Deptford) and she would be thrilled to work at the studios every day and meet loads of famous TV personalities.

Yours, obliged,

D. Armstrong (Mrs.)

P.S. Why bother with a little girl anyway? I suppose it saves you money, but why not use an attractive housewife like the one in the photograph enclosed?

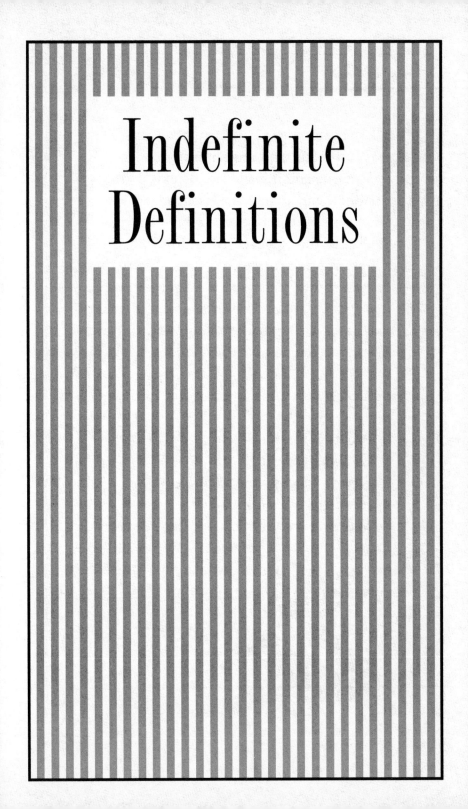

Indefinite Definitions

BRUPT

A brupt is a person
Who is curt and impolite
Brusque and impatient
Who believes he's always right.

A cut-you-off-in-conversation
Interrupting sort.
And short.

CUTE

A cute is sharp
Knows all the angles
Knows exactly how to please.
In a tight corner, no angel
Will squeeze you, this one, by degrees.

DONIS

A donis thinks he's a hulk
Laugh at his bulk and he'll sulk.

ECDOTE

An ecdote will make them laugh
Especially one about you
Therefore it has to be funny
(Though not necessarily true).

GHAST

A ghast is a creature
Who takes a mean delight
In creeping up on children
And giving them a fright.

HEM

A hem, kindly take note
Is a clearing, found not
In the forest, but in the throat.

LERT

A lert sits up straight in class
And pays attention
Lerts are never late for school
Or get detention.

MENDS

A mends is what you make
When in a certain mood
Contrite perhaps
After being rather rude.

PHID

A phid is an insect
That sucks juices from plants
Which is why it is foolish
To grow fuchsias in your pants.

PLOMB

A plomb is someone
Who is very self-possessed
Downright upright
He thinks that he's the best

A stickler for detail
And tight as a drum
Some plombs, I have to say
Are a pain in the bum.

POPLEXY

A poplexy is what happens to people
When they get into a rage
It makes them go all purple
And look three times their age.

SH

A sh is very quiet
(Hold your breath)
Ghostly reminder
Of the way things were
(And will be).

SKEW

A skew is a seabird
With wings of differing sizes
So that when it tries to float
It invariably capsizes.

SPARAGUS

A sparagus is nice for tea.
Plural, not sparaguses – sparagi.

TOMIC

A tomic is extremely small
But splittable
Economic, but not at all
Hospitable.

TROPHY

A trophy not to my taste
Is the one that you're given
When shriven.
Going to waste.

VOID

A void, if I see, smell or hear of
I tend to keep . . . well, clear of.

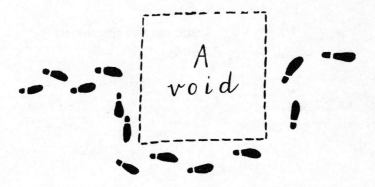

Crocodile Farm

Come wi' me
Down to Crocodile Farm
If you keep your eyes open
You'll come to no harm

There's the old milking shed
Where it's all done by hand
Though we've lost quite a few
As you'll well understand

We make crocodile butter
Yoghurt and cream
Though nobody buys it
It's all lumpy and green

High up on the pastures
They're put out to graze
Where they round up the shepherds
And worry them for days

Then we fatten them up
And kill them humanely
The ones we can catch –
They kill us, mainly

But crocodile meat
Is an acquired taste
A cross between sewage
And stale salmon paste

So I'm giving up crocodiles
Cos my account's in the red
And starting a farm
For alligators instead.

Gigs for Pigs

With the money
that I rake in
from doing
loads of gigs

I'm going to buy up
all the bacon
and give it back
to the pigs.

Peepshow

The ocean's out there
It's vast and it's home
And I want to be in it
With the freedom to roam

Not stuck in a prison
That's made out of glass
For humans to peer into
As they file past

It's all right for goldfish
And smallfry like that
But I deserve more
Than being ogled at

Imagine the look
You'd have on your face
If you had to live
In such a small space

Little wonder
That I look so glum
Banged up in a seaside
Aquarium.

Poor Old Dead Horses

Don't give your rocking-horse
To the old rag and bony

He'll go straight to the knacker
And haggle for money

The stirrups are torn off
The bridle and harness

Chopped up for firewood
It is thrown on the furnace

And the water that boils
Is chucked down the sluices

To wash away what remains
Of poor old dead horses.

Shooting Stars

Under cover of daylight they creep up on us
And on cloudy nights close in, slowly but surely

We are surrounded and outnumbered
If it is clear tonight, take a look for yourself

Notice how they keep still while you are watching
Then, as soon as you blink, they have moved

They think you won't notice but you do
The sinister game of statues they are playing

★ ★ ★

That is why I am out here every night
Rifle in hand, picking them off

Trouble is they are fearless. Kill one
And at the speed of light another takes its place

Aliens with all the time in the world
Licking their lips. Twinkling ever closer.

Life is but a Tree

When the sky is closing in
And the future looks appalling
Remember life is but a tree
Medium-sized and falling.

Keep Your Eyes Peeled

In my field of vision
In that watery field
Grow potatoes with eyes in
Which is why I keep them peeled.

Down to Business

Let's get straight down to business, shall we?
Not waste time on preliminaries.
Coffee before we begin? Are you sure?

Good. Now then, we are both busy people.
So let us address the matter in hand.
Tea? Of course. 'Send in two teas will you?'

You were saying? Was I? Can't stress it
often enough. If time is money, then money is time,
therefore time is the root of all evil.

Gosh, is that the money? We had better
cut the cackle and get down to brass tacks.
Ah, the tea. Help yourself to biscuits.

Now then, where were we? Ah yes,
the biscuits. Sainsbury's I should think,
although Waitrose possibly. Do you really!

I prefer the half-coated chocolate digestive.
Oh no. Plain. Definitely plain.
And jammy dodgers. You know them surely?

Little round ones with . . .

A
Weasel
is Easily
Pleased

A weasel is easily pleased
just give him biscuits
and crumbly cheese

Tickle his whiskers
and if there's a breeze
invite him sailing
and if he agrees

Then it's anchors aweigh
to the Orkneys

. . . Orkneys . . .

The Auk Knees
(and there are two)
are found on a creature
not at all like you

An auk is a bird
(not the bird of prey,
the hawk) but Auk
spelled A-U-K

A seafaring bird
in black and white
that dives for fish
from a tremendous height

Though plump and fat
what amazing speed. Oh
boy, when it moves
it's a feathered torpedo

Then it stands on a rock
all bedraggled and soaked
looking like something
on which the dog choked

On little fat legs
that shiver and freeze
that's where you'll find
the Auk Knees

But where was I?
Of course, I digress
the weasel's the creature
I like best

And mainly because
he's easy to please
just give him biscuits
and crumbly cheese

Grilled lamb chops
and fresh garden peas
all washed down
with peppermint teas

. . . Peppermint teas . . . ?
. . . Pepper minties . . . ?

Aha. Some minties are soft and chewy
others are crunchy and hard
some are crisp as new-laid snow
others as slimy as lard

My grandma ate bowlsful of minties
from morning till night she'd not stop
and she used to sprinkle black pepper
Yes, pepper, all over the top

Now grandad, he preferred humbugs
covered in tomato sauce
or liquorice allsorts in mayonnaise
(but he was nutty of course)

But where was I?
Yes, of course, I apologize
The weasel's the geezer
that gets the prize

For reasons that
he's easy to please
just give him biscuits
and crumbly cheese

Let him climb the Swiss Alps
or the Pyrenees
for winter sports
are a wonderful wheeze

Zoom down the slopes
in and out of the trees
'Look out everybody
a weasel on skis!'

But despite winter sports
at the end of the day
home is the place
that he likes to stay

All warm and cuddly
curled up on your lap
or in front of the fire
when taking a nap

A ball of string
he loves to chase
scampering
all over the place

His eyes are green
his fur is silk
He goes 'miaow'
when it's time for his milk.

Excuse me!

Excuse me, that's not a weasel

No?

No, that's a cat.

It's not a cat. I've got a cat. I keep it in a little cage hanging from the mantelpiece.

A cat in a cage? What does it look like?

It's got wires going this way and that way . . .

No. I mean the cat.

Just like any other cat, I suppose. It's got a little beak, covered in feathers and goes, 'Tweet Tweet.'

Tweet Tweet?

Tweet Tweet.

That's not a cat.

No?

No, that's a canary.

It's not a canary. I've got a canary. I keep it in a kennel in the backyard.

A canary in a kennel? What does it look like?

It's a wooden box with a roof . . .

No, I mean the canary.

Just like any other canary. It's huge, grey, with huge floppy ears, two tusks and a big long trunk.

That's not a canary.

No? What is it, then?

*It's . . . er . . . Why, everybody knows,
it's . . . er . . . you know . . . it's . . . a . . . GOLDFISH!*

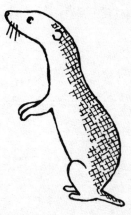

Strangeways

Granny's canary
Escaped from its cage
It's up on the roof
In a terrible rage

Hurling abuse
And making demands
That granny fails
To understand

'Lack of privacy'
'Boring old food'
It holds up placards
Painted and rude

It's not coming down
The canary warns
Till gran carries out
Major reforms.

The message has spread
And now for days
Cage-birds have been acting
In very strange ways.

Home Alone

The church clock chimes midnight
The moon is as white as bone
A cold wind fingers the window
And you're at home alone

Whose shadow is that on the curtain?
A bogeyman? A thief?
Is it a murderer creeping upstairs?
'*No, it's yer Granny, back from the pub.*'

Phew! What a relief.

Customer Service

Last Thursday, the telephone
never stopped ringing.
All day. Never stopped.
Even when I answered it.

So I rang British Telecom
and complained. Told them
it was making my head ache
and would they cut it off.

Sure enough, they sent a man
with an axe, the very next day.
(It's dark down here in the cellar
I wish he'd go away.)

Dear Sir

I was interested in your advert regarding the
post of Controller of Programmes for BBC2.
Although I admit to having little experience of
high-level management, I think that twenty
years as a couch potato qualifies me for serious
consideration.

I must confess that I never watch BBC2 because
I find it dull and over most people's heads. Give
me the commercial channels any day (or night -
joke!), especially cable and Sky. What you need
is someone like me who knows what the average
viewer wants: game shows, funny comedians
and repeats of my favourite gangster movies.
Good television, in other words.

I look forward to hearing from you.

. . . *and on* . . .

Is a slip road
  a road
that is covered in ice?

Are price cuts
  wounds
you get at a price?

Is a waiting room
  a room
that patiently waits?

Is a gate-keeper's
  hobby
collecting gates?

Is a prayer mat
  a carpet
that sings hymns and prays?

Is a horsefly
  a fly
that gallops and neighs?

Does a pony trap
    trap ponies
going to the fair?

Is fire-hose
    stockings
that firemen wear?

Is witchcraft
    jewellery
made by a witch?

Does a battery hen
    cry
when you turn the switch?

When a bricklayer
    lays a brick
what hatches?

Is a scratch team
    so itchy
it scratches?

A Poem about That

I am walking down the street
Thinking about life and beauty
And nature and sex and about
What to have for supper
When he stops me and says:
'Cheer up, it might never happen.'

But already it has.
Because then he says: 'How are you?'
And proceeds to tell me about how he is
And about how he was
And about how he will be
And about
And about
And about
And about
And about
And about
And about
And about
And about an hour later he says:
'I bet you could write a poem about that.'

Trying to Write

Trying to write without a rhyme
Gets more difficult all the time
I wish that I could now reverse
This facility in me verse.

MUCKY

VERY CHEAP

pages and pages of blah

★ **A MUCKY EXCLUSIVE** ★ **A MUCKY EXCLUSIVE** ★

A POEM ABOUT YOU-KNOW-WHAT

At last a poem
  About You-Know-What
It rips off the covers
  And reveals the lot

In at the deep end
  No holds barred
It pulls no punches
  And hits real hard

Not for the squeamish
  Or kids who cry
It's adults only
  And You-Know-Why

No respecter of persons
  Or talking heads
It takes reputations
  And rips them to shreds

Nothing is sacred
  No one is spared
It goes You-Know-Where
  Like no poem has dared

★ ★ ★

(And if you understand
  What it's all about
Would you please give
  You-Know-Who a shout?)

Blah! – Blah blah blah blah

Blah blah blah blah blah
blah blah! Blah, blah blah
blah, 'blah blah blah blah
blah blah blah blah'!

Parrot Fashion

Some learn language
  parrot-fashion
Never learn
  the nitty gritty

The parrot screams
  as Kitty pounces:
'Pretty Polly, Pretty . . .'

The Book Borrower

Seeing it on the shelf
  or by the chair
She seizes it
  and settles down

Ignores my cold stare
  my worried frown
Feels not the rising
  of my hackles

She is immersed
 so deeply
the page crackles

I know what's coming next
  have seen it all before
The novel begun
  is about to become
the novel half read

'Book Borrowers Anonymous'
  I whisper as she makes for the door
She turns: 'Can I borrow it
  until the weekend?'

Never lend, I tell myself
   Never lend. But I weaken
Say 'Of course' and watch her go

I never learn
   I should be firm. Say 'No'
But I haven't the knack

I should give her
   a piece of my mind
But I'd never get it back.

Beguiling

She is so beguiling
That when she beckons
I can run a mile in
Twenty seconds.

Deadpan Delivery

I was sitting down to breakfast
When the doorbell rang. Brrr. Brrr.
Muesli with banana sliced in. Brrr. Brrr.
Toast and coffee. Brrr. Brrr. Brrr.
(Yes, it was freezing cold)

Wrapping my dressing-gown
Tightly round me, I opened the door.
It was the deadpan man with a delivery.
'What is it this time?' I asked.
'That's nothing, you should see my wife.'

He quipped. Deadpan.

The Dada Christmas
Catalogue

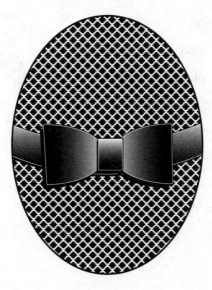

1. A chocolate comb
2. Can-of-worms opener
3. Two non-stick frying-pans
4. Sticky frying-pan
5. A book-end
6. Abrasive partridges
7. Reversible fridge
8. Nervous door handles
9. Pair of non-secateurs
10. Day-glo Tipp-Ex
11. An underwater ashtray
12. Pencil polish
13. Pair of socks, identical but for the colour
14. A pit stop
15. Jar of tarantula jam

16. Contact lens adhesive
17. Shattered window-pane jigsaw puzzle
18. One stereophonic earphone
19. A computer buff
20. Nasal floss (unwaxed)21.
21. Magnetic cutlery
22. A hip joint
23. A groovy cartilage
24. Three-way mirror
25. Tape measure
26. Tape worm
27. A shadow of its former self
28. Reusable sellotape (sticky on both sides)
29. Spare mushroom
30. Not a pipe.

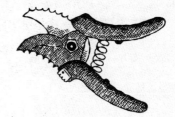

Made to Measure

Lenny, a good tailor? Lenny?
You bet. Master craftsman. Good as any
in Savile Row. Measure you up
for a suit soon as look at you

Out comes the tape. A lasso
Notching up haloes in the air
(Chinese noodle-chefs, off-duty
gather enviously and stare)

Inside leg, chest and knee
accurate to the nth degree.
'Walk this way, sir, it's a pleasure.'
Lenny? Why, he was made to measure.

Cobblers

'Footing the Bill'
is the name of the shop
that repairs the boots
of the British cop.

Snail's Pace

a snail's face
is not one I'd like to kiss
a snail's pace
g o e s   s o m e t h i n g   r a t h e r   l i k e   t h i s
and as for that shell suit!

The Figment Tree

I believe in fairies
And each Sunday after tea
At the bottom of the garden
Beneath the figment tree
Alone, I sit and wonder
If they believe in me.

Riddle

I'm older than my eldest son
But younger than my mother
One ear has an eagle tattooed on
Skull and crossbones on the other
What am I?

The Outlaw's In-laws

An outlaw's mother
And mother-in-law
Went riding down
In Witchita

The latter, without
A trace of remorse
Pushed the former
Off her horse

Now the outlaw's mother
Is stiff as a board
And the outlaw's mother-
in-law, outlawed.

Hill of Beans

'Life ain't nuttin' but a hill o' beans,'
drawled Granma, and removing
her corncob pipe, spat a stream
of baccy juice into the empty firegrate
before settling back with a jug of bourbon
into her old rocking chair

To think, only this time last year
she was working for the Welsh Water Authority.

Famous Last Words

(No. 73) KING HAROLD:
'I spy with my little . . . . . . ouch.'

(No. 49) KING HENRY I:
'No thanks, another lamprey and I'll
burst.
OK, just the one.'

(No. 81) TYRANNOSAURUS REX:
'Looks like rain.'

(No. 114) KIT MARLOWE:
'Step outside and say that.'

(No. 4) GENERAL CUSTER:
'Let's go kick ass.'

(No. 53) WILLIAM TELL JR:
'Great, Dad, now try it with a radish.'

(No. 36) AGATHA CHRISTIE:
'It was agghhhh . . . '

(No. 8066) LORD NELSON:
'Bless me, Hardy.'

Dear Sir or Madam
I wish to apply
For the post as Po-
etry Editor

At Viking Puffin.
I have been writing
Verse for many years
So far without suc-

cess. The position
Therefore would give me
A wonderful opp-
ortunity to

See myself in print.
I look forward to
An early reply.
Yours faithfully etc.

Sylvia Tendrill

Everything Touches

Everything touches, life interweaves
Starlight and gunsmoke, ashes and leaves
Birdsong and thunder, acid and rain
Everything touches, unbroken chain

Chainsaw and rainbow, warrior and priest
Assassin off-duty, beauty and beast
Heartbeat and hightide, ebb and flow
Cardboard cathedral covered in snow

Snowdrop and gangrene, hangman and clown
Walls that divide come tumbling down
Seen through the night the glimmer of day
Light is but darkness worn away

Past and future, distance and time
Atom to atom, water to wine
Look all around, what do you see?
Everything touches, you're touching me

Look all around, what do you see?
Everything touches, you're touching me.

. . . and on.

Is sandpaper
  used
for wrapping up sand?

If you lay down
  your arms
can you still lend a hand?

Is a sick bed
  a bed
that is feeling unwell?

Is a crime wave
  a criminal's
wave of farewell?

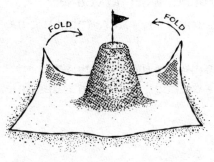

Is a cop shop
    a shop
where you can purchase a cop?

Is the last laugh
    the long one
before the big drop?

Is a bent copper
    a policeman
who has gone round the bend?

Is the bottom line
    the line
on your bottom?   The End.

Index of First Lines